Contents

Making a difference	2
Some apples, please?	4
How to run a Great Book Swap	7
One Million Paws Walk	10
Ryan's well	12
Strands in action	16

Making a difference

People are happiest when they are giving, they are saddest when they are just taking. And that is the core message of community. Kevin Rudd, former Australian prime minister

Sometimes people need help. For whatever reason, life isn't going well for them. But because we live in a **community** where people help others in need, help is never far away.

In every community, there are people who **participate** in groups that help others in need. Some of these groups are highly organised and have lots of **volunteers**.

Participating in a project or with a group to help others or the environment is a great thing to do. It not only makes other people's lives easier or protects the environment, but it also makes you feel good. There are lots of different ways you can make a difference in someone's life.

Did you know?

Make a Wish is a community group that **grants** the wishes of very sick children. Since Make a Wish started in Australia in 1980, it has granted more than 7000 wishes. Make a Wish has more than 1000 volunteers who help to raise money to grant wishes.

community a group of people who live in the same area
participate to take part in
volunteers people who do something for no pay
grants allows or gives

LET'S FIND OUT

- What is a community?
- Why might some people in a community need help?
- Which groups in your community help others?
- Why do you think some people help others or help to protect the environment?
- How can you participate in groups that help others or the environment?

These people are taking part in a fun run to raise money for charity.

Some apples, please?

Walsh Street Primary School
50 Walsh Street
Katandra WA 6999

Your Friendly Greengrocer
80 Leila Road
Katandra WA 6999

27 September

Dear Sir or Madam,
As part of our **fundraising** this year, we have decided to collect money to **donate** to a **charity**. The charity buys presents to give to children who don't have a lot. The gifts are given to the kids on their birthday. We estimate $200 will buy a lot of presents for these kids.

On 15 October, our school is holding our annual Spring Sports Carnival. We want to sell slinky apples for $1 each at the carnival to raise the money.

fundraising raising money for a purpose
donate give
charity a group that helps people in need

We need 200 apples to sell, because 200 apples sold for $1 each equals $200! Would you be able to help us by donating 200 of your delicious apples? Our teacher, Ms Flanagan, has said she can pick up the apples in her car.

By helping us, you'd be helping these children get a birthday present. The thought that even one child doesn't receive a birthday present makes us feel really sad. We all get presents on our birthdays, so we want to make sure that these kids get one, too.

Yours sincerely,
Year 3F students at Walsh Street Primary School

Breakaway tasks

Remembering

1 How much money does Year 3F at Walsh Street Primary School want to raise?

2 Where does Year 3F intend to sell the apples?

Understanding

3 Explain to a partner why Year 3F needs the money.

Applying

4 What gifts would you buy for $200? Research prices and write a list.

Analysing

5 Research to find out how a slinky apple machine works. Draw a picture showing your findings.

6 Brainstorm and write down five other ways the class could raise the money.

Evaluating

7 Do you think the greengrocer will donate the apples? Give three reasons for your opinion and discuss with a partner.

8 Survey the class on whether 3F will raise the money, and include why or why not. Prepare a graph.

Creating

9 Write a reply to Year 3F from Your Friendly Greengrocer.

10 Design a poster that the class could use at the sports carnival to help sell the slinky apples.

How to run a Great Book Swap

The Great Book Swap raises money to buy books for Aboriginal and Torres Strait Islander people who live in remote communities. It is organised by the Indigenous Literacy Foundation. Here's how to run one at your school.

Aim

- To raise money for the Indigenous Literacy Foundation, so it can buy new books for Aboriginal and Torres Strait Islander people

What you need

- A large room
- Lots of tables
- Bookplates and pens
- Books to swap
- A container for money

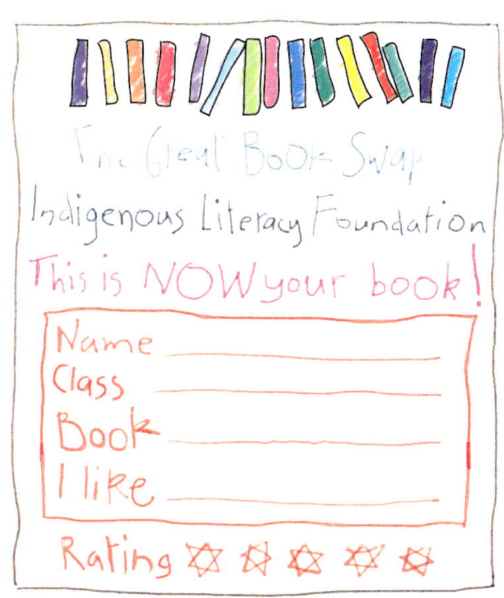

An example of a bookplate

What to do

1 Register your school on the Indigenous Literacy Foundation website.
2 Choose a day to hold your swap.
3 Create a Great Book Swap bookplate, so people can rate or say why they liked this book. Make lots of copies.

---

remote far away
literacy being able to read and write
register to add your name and details to a list

4 Before the swap, ask everyone to bring a book they loved reading, but don't mind giving away. Have them fill in a bookplate.
5 Sort through the books. Put them into **categories**.
6 Organise activities for the day, such as readings from books, or a visit from an author.

On the Book Swap day

1 Set up the tables. Set out the books in the categories.
2 Invite people to put $2 in the container in exchange for a book.
3 At the end of the day, send the money collected to the Indigenous Literacy Foundation. This must be done by 1 December.

Students from the remote Yakanarra Community School in the Kimberley region of Western Australia

categories groups

Breakaway tasks

Remembering

1 Who organises the Great Book Swap?

2 In your own words, what is the aim of the Great Book Swap?

Understanding

3 Where could you hold the swap? Draw a diagram of possible places in your school.

Applying

4 Think of a book you would donate. Discuss with a partner why it was one of your favourite books and why other people would like it.

5 Find part of your favourite book to read on swap day. Practise your reading, and then read it to the class.

Analysing

6 Persuade your teacher to get involved in the Great Book Swap. Work in groups and prepare a short speech.

7 What categories would you sort books into? Draw pictures for each category.

Evaluating

8 With a partner, list other ways you could raise money for the Indigenous Literacy Foundation.

Creating

9 Design your own bookplate for your book swap.

10 Design a radio or TV ad for the book swap.

Poem

One Million Paws Walk

Amelia and her dog Prince took part in the Million Paws Walk and raised $68. She wrote this poem after the walk. The Million Paws Walk raises money, so the RSPCA can care for the many animals that enter their shelters every year and find them new homes.

One Million Paws Walk
By Amelia

Large and small,
Short and tall,
They came and they walked,
And I saw them all!
But did I see one million paws?
I'm not sure,
I'm not sure.

So I decided to count them,
And they all stood still –
No more jumping and bumping,
Nor dancing and prancing!
And there really were one million paws,
Of that I'm sure,
Of that I'm sure!

RSPCA the Royal Society for the Prevention (stopping) of Cruelty to Animals
shelters places that provide protection

Breakaway tasks

Remembering

1 How much money did Amelia raise for the RSPCA?

2 What does the RSPCA do?

Understanding

3 Do you think Amelia's dog is a male or female? Give a reason for your answer.

Applying

4 Fill in an Our five senses chart about the Million Paws Walk.

5 Research the RSPCA and write a fact file about it.

Analysing

6 Explain how Amelia managed to count the paws on the walk.

7 Suggest other verbs to describe what the dogs would be doing on the walk.

Evaluating

8 Is the Million Paws Walk a good way for the RSPCA to raise money? Evaluate the walk using a PMI chart.

Creating

9 Write a narrative about an animal rescued by the RSPCA that finds a new home. Write it from the point of view of the animal.

10 In groups, write and perform a play about a group of friends who go on the Million Paws Walk.

Ryan's well

Ryan Hreljac, aged 17

Ryan Hreljac began raising money when he was six years old. He wanted to build a well in Africa, so people would have clean water like he did in Canada. At first, he thought he only had to raise $70, but he found out it would cost $2000 to build the well!

It took Ryan a long time to raise the money, but he did it. Since then, he has raised millions of dollars for water and sanitation projects in Africa.

It was a tough day for Grade 1 pupil Ryan Hreljac. He had just learned some upsetting news.

His teacher had been talking to the class about problems facing people in other parts of the world. One of the most serious problems, she told them, was the lack of safe drinking water. Bad water was causing thousands and thousands of people, including children, to become sick and even die.

well a hole dug in the ground to get water

sanitation projects projects to improve public health by encouraging clean and healthy practices

These children from Africa are getting water from a well.

"That's crazy," Ryan thought. In his house, he could use as much water as he wanted. And on top of that, the teacher said, people had to walk as far as 20 kilometres every day in search of water.

It took a while for it all to sink in. The teacher told them that in Africa it cost only $70 to build a well that could supply a village and surrounding areas with safe, clean water.

That was it! Ryan would ask his parents for the $70 and, problem solved.

Hmmm, not so fast. Ryan would have to earn the money. His parents would give him **chores** around the house and pay him for his work. If he really wanted to build a well in Africa, he would have to prove it by working for it.

Ryan worked and worked. After four months of chores, Ryan had a cookie tin filled with $70 in coins…

chores jobs or tasks

Breakaway tasks

Remembering

1 How much money did Ryan first think it cost to build a well in Africa?

2 How did Ryan earn $70?

3 How much money did it actually cost to build a well?

Understanding

4 Make a list of 10 things Ryan might have done around the house to earn the money.

5 Draw or trace a map of the world. Colour in and label Africa and Australia.

Applying

6 Research Ryan's life and write a profile about him.

Analysing

7 Work with a partner to identify the problems with water in Africa. Compare these with where you live.

8 Why do you think it is a good idea to build wells in Africa? In a group, brainstorm some ideas on how you could raise money to build wells in Africa.

Evaluating

9 How do you think Ryan would have felt when he was later told that he needed to raise $2000 not $70? Make a list of adjectives describing his feelings.

Creating

10 Work in small groups to write a news report on what Ryan achieved. Film this or present it to the class.

Strands in action

Core tasks

1 Research a group in your local community that your class could help. Prepare an oral presentation with information about:
- what the group does and its aims
- how long the group has been running and who started it
- ways in which your class could participate.

2 Organise an event that will make a difference to other people or the environment.
- Plan the event. Include how it will help.
- Present your ideas to the class.
- As a class, vote on the best idea.

Extra tasks

1 Design a poster to encourage students to take part in the Million Paws Walk.

2 Write a letter to Ryan Hreljac, thanking him for raising money for projects in Africa.

3 Survey five people about the things they have done to make a difference to others, or to protect the environment. What was the most common thing? What was the least common? Include a graph.

4 Write an acrostic poem about an activity you took part in to help your community.

When you are writing a rhyming poem, make a list of rhyming words about your topic.